AF131387

BOOK ANALYSIS

By Corinne Herward

The Yellow Wallpaper

BY CHARLOTTE PERKINS GILMAN

Bright
≡Summaries.com

CHARLOTTE PERKINS GILMAN

AMERICAN NOVELIST AND SHORT STORY WRITER

- **Born in Hartford in 1860.**
- **Died in Pasadena in 1935.**
- **Notable works:**
  - *Women and Economics: A Study of the Economic Relation Between Men and Women as a Factor in Social Evolution* (1898), non-fiction
  - *Herland* (1915), novel
  - *With Her in Ourland* (1916), novel

Charlotte Perkins Gilman was born in Connecticut and grew up in poverty after her father abandoned his family. She spent much of her childhood with her father's aunts, including Harriet Beecher Stowe (American writer and social activist, 1811-1896), the author of *Uncle Tom's Cabin* (1852). Gilman married Charles Walter Stetson in 1884 and had one daughter.

Gilman suffered a serious case of post-partum depression, which was dismissed as a nervous or hysterical complaint by her husband and doctors. Gilman left her husband soon afterwards, although she did not obtain an official divorce until 1894. She embarked on a relationship with a woman named Adeline Knapp, which Gilman found far more fulfilling than her heterosexual marriage. Their relationship ultimately ended, and Gilman later found love with her cousin, Houghton Gilman.

Charlotte Perkins Gilman was a writer who was preoccupied with gender and its impact on the lives of women around her. Influenced by her experience of post-partum depression, Gilman commenced work on *The Yellow Wallpaper* in 1890. The dark account of mental captivity encapsulates the damaging effects of the lack of autonomy offered to women of Gilman's generation. A feminist icon, Gilman's unique grasp of gender and the structures it enforces ensure that her work remains relevant in the modern world.

THE YELLOW WALLPAPER

A CHILLING PSYCHOLOGICAL DIARY

- **Genre:** short story
- **Reference edition:** Perkins Gilman, C. (2008) *The Yellow Wallpaper*. [Online]. Urbana: Project Gutenberg. [Accessed 27 January 2019]. Available from: <http://www.gutenberg.org/files/1952/1952-h/1952-h.htm>
- **1st edition:** 1892
- **Themes:** depression, domestic life, gender, independence, mental captivity

The Yellow Wallpaper is the first-person account of a woman suffering from a mental illness. Her husband, who is also her doctor, disregards her complaints and prescribes her what was known as 'a rest cure'. This involved living as domestic a life as possible, reading very little, and never writing or visiting anyone. Therefore, the setting of the book is a room with barred windows at the top of a colonial mansion, where the protagonist is surrounded by the titular yellow wallpaper: "It is dull enough to confuse the eye in following, pronounced enough to constantly irritate, and provoke study, and when you follow the lame, uncertain curves for a little distance they suddenly commit suicide" (p. 2). John, the narrator's husband, is an authoritarian figure, an unsettling gender dynamic that characterised the marriages of Gilman's era. John belittles the narrator's suffering, undermines her wishes to go out and see people, and utterly controls her. Without any activity to occupy her except staring at the yellow wallpaper, the protagonist begins to see a figure inside the paper, and imagines that it is a woman crawling around, trying to get out. In the final day of the narrator's captivity she is driven to tearing the wallpaper from the walls to free the woman in the paper. John walks in on her, and she cries "I've got out of you at last [...] in spite of you and Jane" (p. 7). John faints, and the narrator continues crawling around the room in a warped embodiment of the figure in the wallpaper.

SUMMARY

IMPRISONMENT AND INDISPOSITION

At the beginning of the story the narrator and her husband John have decided to rent a colonial mansion for the summer months. This is an exceptional circumstance for the ordinary, middle-class couple, the narrator explains, and at the beginning of the story she revels in its isolation. "A colonial mansion, a hereditary estate, I would say a haunted house, and reach the height of romantic felicity – but that would be asking too much of fate!" (p. 1). This allusion to the supernatural foreshadows the strange and twisted events of the story as the narrator later spirals into madness. It is unclear what the narrator's mental state is at the beginning of the story, but her rational objection to her 'medicine' and her genuine affection for her prescriptive husband John, as well as her baby, hint that she is depressed, but not insane. "I did write for a while, in spite of them;" Gilman's narrator explains, "but it does exhaust me a good deal – having to be so sly about it, or else meet with heavy opposition" (*ibid*.).

The mental captivity and suppression of her personality weighs on the narrator, and the fact that her husband is also her physician means that her imprisonment is total. The narrator does write sporadically in the diary that we are reading, but it is hidden the instant her husband or his sister appear. John also chooses the narrator's bedroom, a circumstance that infuriates her: "I wanted one downstairs that opened on the piazza and had roses all over the window and such pretty old-fashioned chintz hangings!" (p. 2). John refuses to grant her request because he would not be able to fit a second bed in the room or monitor the narrator during the night. Instead he installs her in the former nursery, a large, airy room with revolting musty yellow wallpaper. The narrator complains:

> "One of those sprawling flamboyant patterns committing every artistic sin. It is dull enough to confuse the eye in following, pronounced enough to constantly irritate, and provoke study, and when you follow the lame, uncertain curves

for a little distance they suddenly commit suicide – plunge off at outrageous angles, destroy
themselves in unheard-of contradictions." (*ibid.*)

This description weaves the narrator's path with
the wallpaper, entwining their dull and simul-
taneously outrageous progress.

DETERIORATION AND DEPRESSION

Two weeks later the narrator picks up her pen,
explaining that she has not felt like writing since
her first night in the house. John has left her
alone almost every day and is often away during
the night as well, as his other cases are so serious.
"I am glad my case is not serious!" the narrator
half-sarcastically remarks, "But these nervous
troubles are dreadfully depressing" (*ibid.*). The
woman in the story frets about her inability to
be a comfort to her husband, concerned that
she is a failure as a wife and as a mother: "Such
a dear baby!" the narrator exclaims wistfully,
"And yet I cannot be with him, it makes me so
nervous" (*ibid.*). Yet the narrator is also aware
that her husband is unable to empathise with
her condition: "I suppose John never was nervous
in all his life. He laughs at me so about this

wallpaper!" (*ibid*.). Although her husband at first assures her that he will remove the paper that agitates the author, he changes his mind and decides that it would be worse to give into her whims. John tells his wife that if he did get rid of the wallpaper, she would then complain about the bed being nailed to the floor, or the bars on the windows, and the author admits that these features of the room do bother her. The bars and the bed are controlled, hemmed in and shut down, indicative of the prison the author is enduring. John constantly demands that the narrator exercise more self-control, and while she likes to look out of the window and imagine people walking up and down the paths, he tells her to shut up her imagination as it is dangerous to her sensitive mental condition. Despite her fatigue, the author longs to see her friends Cousin Henry and Julia, and her husband promises that when she is better, they can come. At present, John says, he would as soon put fireworks in her pillowcase as to have such 'stimulating' people around his wife. The narrator sees John's sister, Jennie, who is also their housekeeper, coming towards the house and hurries to put away her writing before she sees it: "Such a dear girl as she is and so careful of me! I must not let her find me writing" (*ibid*.). As she finishes writing the author looks at the wallpaper, and as the sun shines on it she sees the outline of a sulking figure behind the swirling pattern. The narrator stops writing abruptly as she hears John's sister coming up the stairs.

BREAKDOWN

Summer wears on in the colonial mansion and the narrator still feels sick and depressed. John begins to threaten the narrator with Weir Mitchell, Gilman's real-life physician. "I had a friend who was in his hands once and she says he is just like John and my brother, only more so!" the narrator frets (p. 3). The narrator's deteriorating mental state is characterised by her preoccupation with the yellow wallpaper, and her main occupation is tracing its swirling pattern around the room for hours on end. Even writing is becoming too much for the author, as she claims that in some ways it is a huge relief to her, but that often the effort overcomes the relief. In a desperate effort, the narrator begs John to let her go and visit Cousin Henry and Julia, but John refuses, and as the narrator bursts into tears at this, her hysteria confirms John's belief that she is unwell. The narrator is once again confined to the nursery, but she is thankful that she is there and not her baby.

The author confesses that she sees a woman behind the wallpaper, and that she stoops and creeps around the room. The narrator asks John again if they can leave, but he refuses, as their lease is not up for another three weeks, and he believes that the narrator is getting better. The narrator rejects this claim, but John is annoyed, and then decides to laugh at her concern. "Bless her little heart," John says, "she shall be as sick as she pleases" (p. 5). The narrator stays up all night watching the wallpaper after these remarks, imagining the bars that run down the pattern, and the figure subdued behind them. By day, the pattern is unclear, but by moonlight, the narrator claims, the image is obvious. Days wear on, and John makes the narrator lie down during the day more frequently. She cannot sleep, however, and spends her time trying to discern the figure in the paper instead.

With a week left in their stay, the author says that she does not want to leave, she needs to know what she has been studying. The smell of the wallpaper pervades the house and the author's clothes, and she has noticed a long streak around the skirting board, as if someone had crawled around the room. She sees the woman behind the paper shaking her bars, but she feels that nobody could get out from such a strangling pattern. The narrator locks the door now to be alone with the wallpaper, and she creeps around the room. On the last day in the house the narrator begins to tear the paper from the wall. Jennie sees what she has done and is shocked, but the narrator lies and says she did it out of spite at the ugly nasty paper, and Jennie agrees that she would not mind tearing it up either. The narrator tells Jennie not to disturb her, and locks the door, throwing the key down into the front path. She then gnaws at the nailed down bed and pulls off as much of the paper as she can. She becomes so frustrated that she wants to jump out of the window, but she knows her motivation would not be understood. She sees dozens of women now, all crawling around, and, frightened, she ties herself up with a piece of rope. She knows that when daytime comes, she will have to get back inside the wallpaper. John arrives home and enters the room to find the narrator crawling around the floor. "I've got out at last," the narrator says, "in spite of you and Jane!" (p. 7). John faints, and the story ends as the narrator continues around the room, crawling over John's inert body.

CHARACTER STUDY

THE NARRATOR

Based on Gilman, the nameless narrator is the dominant voice of the text. A young wife who recently had a baby, the narrator suffers from post-partum depression and is unable to be around her young child because of the anxiety it gives her. The narrator loves her controlling husband John, and she does her utmost to obey his wishes, although she says she disagrees with the treatment he prescribes. The narrator keeps a secret diary which acts as a window into her mind as her behaviour begins to spiral. We see her captivity frustrate her active mind, and she begins to imagine that there is a woman in the wallpaper. Although the narrator wishes to leave the house and the room during the first half of the story, there is a marked shift as her mental health deteriorates, leading her to voice a desire to stay in the room and discover what the wallpaper means. In a break with sanity, the narrator decides to tear away the wallpaper and release the woman, or women, that are trapped inside its pattern. "I've got out at last [...] in spite of you and Jane", the narrator ultimately gloats to her husband (p. 7). Although some critics argue that this is an allusion to Jane Eyre (the protagonist of the 1847 novel of the same name), or is a garbled version of John's sister Jennie, others suggest that this is the narrator's name, and she recognises that she has been an obstacle to change.

JOHN

John is a doctor, and as the narrator's husband he prescribes her what is known as a rest cure, where the narrator is forced not to read or write or see anybody exciting, and in short stay at home and be quiet. John firmly believes in the efficacy of this cure and is irritated by his wife's insistence that she is not getting better. He repeatedly infantilises his wife, referring to her as "a blessed little goose", "a little girl", and other juvenile terms of endearment (p. 5). John never takes his wife's opinion into consideration and is an extremely authoritarian figure. He refuses to allow his wife to choose her own bedroom and prioritises his comfort above hers. John is also often manipulative, and he makes his wife feel guilty for her depression. He is, some critics have argued, merely a figure of his time and victim of the era he was born into, but that does not make his actions less damaging to the narrator or any of the 19th-century victims of oppression.

JENNIE

Jennie is John's sister and is associated with domesticity, providing a juxtaposition to the narrator. The narrator is perplexed by the fact that Jennie does not seem to aspire to any loftier station than that of her brother's housekeeper, and finds her to be very sweet, if not substantial. Yet Jennie also plays an active role in the narrator's imprisonment and supervises her strictly: "I must not let her find me writing," the narrator worries (p. 2). Jennie also perceives the narrator's fascination with the wallpaper and confronts her about the yellow streaks found on her and John's clothing. In the final act of the story, Jennie discovers that the narrator has begun to tear the wallpaper off the walls, and asks her what she has been doing in shock. However, when the narrator replies light-heartedly that she does not like the paper and just wanted to tear it out of spite, Jennie is deceived and agrees that it is disagreeable. Jennie allows the narrator to skip dinner and sleep alone instead of watching her, allowing for the breach in the narrator's sanity.

MARY

Mary is the narrator's nurse and tends very carefully to her baby. She is never present in the nursery where the narrator is staying, but she acts as a reminder of the narrator's domestic and maternal failure. In Christian cultures, the name Mary has connotations of the Virgin Mary, a symbol of idealised femininity and purity.

THE WOMAN IN THE WALLPAPER

Arguably the most important character in *The Yellow Wallpaper*, the woman who dwells in the swirling pattern is representative of 19th-century women who were imprisoned in the domestic sphere. At times the figure in the wallpaper is one woman and at times she is many. She is clearest to the narrator at night time, and while John sleeps the narrator can see this woman shaking the bars of the yellow paper, trying to get out. The narrator recognises the impossibility of getting out of a wallpaper that cuts off one route and then another, hemming the woman in. As the narrator's mental health deteriorates, she imagines that she too is behind the wallpaper, a secret blot on John's domestic happiness. The 'creeping' that the narrator and the woman in the wallpaper engage in is suggestive of the secretive nature of their rebellion against imprisonment and their inability to assert their identity in the public sphere.

ANALYSIS

FIRST-PERSON NARRATION

The first-person narration in *The Yellow Wallpaper* immerses the reader in the mental turmoil of our protagonist. Her frustration becomes ours as we recognise that her valid concerns about her mental health are being dismissed by those around her. The fragmented nature of the narration adds to the sense of control and imprisonment, with the sections of Gilman's short story becoming more urgent as the narrative and her insanity progress. Although stream of consciousness is not present in the first half of the story, Gilman implements it gradually in order to depict the narrator's insanity. The unstructured thoughts thrown down on paper mirror the frenzied actions and illogical thought processes of the narrator as she becomes determined to set her mind free. The narrator personifies her depression and confinement in the wallpaper, noting that even when she is out of the nursery, she can turn her head and smell the odour of the wallpaper hanging over her, an ever-present oppression. The gaps in the author's writing also provoke curiosity and imagination about the events in the house that the narrator does not tell us about. This is indicated through the first two journal entries, which are dated two weeks apart, as the narrator tells us that she has not felt like writing. This disinterest is an early indication of her deteriorating mental state and it also shows that the later loss of interest in anything other than the wallpaper, her disinclination to leave the house and her separation from company are unhealthy signs of a mind imprisoned. Although the narrator is originally disgusted by the wallpaper, Gilman weaves the woman in the wallpaper into the narrator's story as an element of her subconscious, clearest at night when she is supposed to be sleeping. While the narrator's mind is crumbling, she associates herself with the woman in the wallpaper and at the end of the story their identities converge, as the narrator says that she has escaped the wallpaper, that she is free, and crawls around her fallen husband.

FEMININE FIGURES

There are four women in *The Yellow Wallpaper*: the narrator, the woman in the wallpaper, Mary the nursery maid and Jennie the housekeeper. All of these women are placed in the private sphere, which was the only part of life that women were allowed to occupy in 19th-century society. As a result, women's voices were seldom heard in art or politics, and many talented women were stifled under the oppression. Later in the story, Gilman undermines the individuality of the narrator's story, as critics such as Karen Ford have remarked (Ford, 1985: 309). Flat and unoriginal names such as John and Mary add further credence to a reading of the narrator's story as a reflection of the lives of many women who were driven insane by their imprisonment in a life that they did not want. The narrator's attempts to socialise with 'Cousin Henry and Julia', and therefore socialise with exciting people beyond her husband and son, run counter to the expectations of domesticity that pervaded in Gilman's time. The fact that the narrator's prison is a nursery is indicative of the impact that child-rearing conventions have had on her sanity. The conversations that John has with his wife reinforce her pigeon-holed existence, as he diminishes her importance, calls her a 'goose' and constantly presumes to know more about her mental health than she does. Meanwhile, the narrator is haunted by the women that have taken her position as the heads of the household, Mary and Jennie. Mary, who is described as "so good with the baby" (p. 2) is meant to relieve the narrator's anxiety, yet she often frets about her inability to be around her child and her nervousness about her failure. Jennie, who is her sister-in-law, is "a perfect and enthusiastic housekeeper and hopes for no better profession" (p. 3). Their contented resignation to their domestic pursuits provides a contrast with the narrator whose imagination, once confined, becomes twisted and injures her. Lastly, the woman in the wallpaper, who represents women's imprisonment, is a manifold figure. Once the narrator begins to set her free, she finds other women whose subjugated identity 'creeps' around the patriarchal space.

NIGHT AND DAY

In literature, daylight and the sun have traditionally been associated with masculine energy while night and moonlight are more typically understood as feminine symbols. Gilman adapts these dichotomies in *The Yellow Wallpaper*, inverting the power of the public and the private and asserting a type of feminine power through the night time passages. During the day John micromanages the narrator's life down to a quarter of an hour, prescribing exercise and rest, but never giving her time to sit and think. This is his sphere of control, and he exercises it to its fullest extent, dominating the narrator utterly. However, when John sleeps the narrator is free to think, and her imagination is released as her mind turns over the question of the wallpaper, determined to rationalise it. During the day the narrator even attempts to impose John's rationality on the wallpaper, deciding to categorise it in terms of design principals: "I know that this thing was not arranged on any laws of radiation, or alternation, or repetition, or symmetry, or anything else that I ever heard of," the narrator complains as she begins to puzzle out the lines (p. 3). The narrator ultimately resigns herself to the irrationality of the wallpaper, and the fact that its formless, shapeless expression will haunt her. In the daylight the woman in the wallpaper is passive and motionless, which correlates to the narrator's own daytime activities. However, at night, the narrator tells us, when the moonlight shines through the window, she can see the figure in the wallpaper shaking the bars of her cage, asking to be let out. The woman in the wallpaper also creeps around, a strange half-ashamed motion which Gilman suggests is the fate of any woman trying to express themselves in the patriarchal sphere. The allusions to night and the subconscious intertwine the plight of the woman in the wallpaper with that of the narrator and allow her to recognise her own despair as she resolves to free both herself and the woman in the wallpaper from their respective prisons.

FURTHER REFLECTION

SOME QUESTIONS TO THINK ABOUT...

- Do you think the narrator's decline was an inevitable mental illness, or could it have been avoided? Explain why you think it could or could not have been prevented.
- Charlotte Perkins Gilman wrote *The Yellow Wallpaper* as a result of her own experience of post-partum depression. Do you think that the story is a realistic depiction of mental illness?
- In *The Yellow Wallpaper* the protagonist undergoes what was known as 'a rest cure', where writing was given up and women were encouraged to live as domestic a life as possible. Do you think that sexism played a role in the imposition of rest cures?
- John, the narrator's husband, believes that he knows what is best for the narrator and never follows her wishes. Is John a villain, or does he simply not understand his wife? Explain why or why not.

- Is the end of *The Yellow Wallpaper* tragic or is it a satisfying liberation? Explain what you think the end of the story means.
- Write 5-6 lines on what could happen after John wakes up and finds his wife crawling around the room. Do you think he would send her to Weir Mitchell, the psychologist? Do you think she can recover? Explain the reasoning behind your theory of what could happen next.
- The dichotomy of night and day is one way the tensions between male and female are explored in the story. Why do you think the narrator feels imprisoned during the day, even when John is absent?
- Who is the woman in the wallpaper? Do you think she represents the narrator, or is she a general figure of mistreated 19th-century women? How do you think her representation contrasts with Charlotte Brontë's (English writer, 1816-1855) woman in the attic in her 1847 novel *Jane Eyre*?

We want to hear from you!
Leave a comment on your online library
and share your favourite books on social media!

FURTHER READING

REFERENCE EDITION

- Perkins Gilman, C. (2008) *The Yellow Wallpaper*. [Online]. Urbana: Project Gutenberg. [Accessed 27 January 2019]. Available from: <http://www.gutenberg.org/files/1952/1952-h/1952-h.htm>

REFERENCE STUDIES

- Ford, K. (1985) "The Yellow Wallpaper" and Women's Discourse. *Tulsa Studies in Women's Literature*. 4(2), pp. 309-314.

- (No date) The Yellow Wallpaper. *Wikipedia*. [Online]. [Accessed 3 February 2019]. Available from: <https://en.wikipedia.org/wiki/The_Yellow_Wallpaper>

ADDITIONAL SOURCES

- Bates Dock, J. (1996) "But One Expects That": Charlotte Perkins Gilman's "The Yellow Wallpaper" and the Shifting Light of Scholarship. *PMLA Modern Language Association*. 111(1), pp. 52-65.

- Davis, C. (2010) *Charlotte Perkins Gilman: A Biography*. Stanford: Stanford University Press.

- Perkins Gilman, C. (1998) *The Abridged Diaries of Charlotte Perkins Gilman*. Denise D. Knight (ed). Virginia: University Press of Virginia.

ADAPTATIONS

- The Yellow Wallpaper. *Suspense*. (1957) [Radio show episode]. William N. Robson. Dir. US: CBS.

- The Yellow Wallpaper. *Fear on Four*. (1990) [Radio show episode]. UK: BBC.

- *The Yellow Wallpaper*. (2015) [One-woman how]. US: Central Works of Berkeley.

www.brightsummaries.com

Ebook EAN: 9782808017947

Paperback EAN: 9782808017954

Legal Deposit: D/2019/12603/64

Cover: © Primento

Digital conception by Primento, the digital partner of publishers.